Mel Bay Presents

Mariachi Favorites
for Solo Guitar

Arranged by Laura Sobrino
Adapted for Classical Guitar by Steve Eckels

MEL BAY ®

1 2 3 4 5 6 7 8 9 0

Visit us on the Web at www.melbay.com — E-mail us at email@melbay.com

Table of Contents

El llano grande

P.D./adapted by Steve Eckels

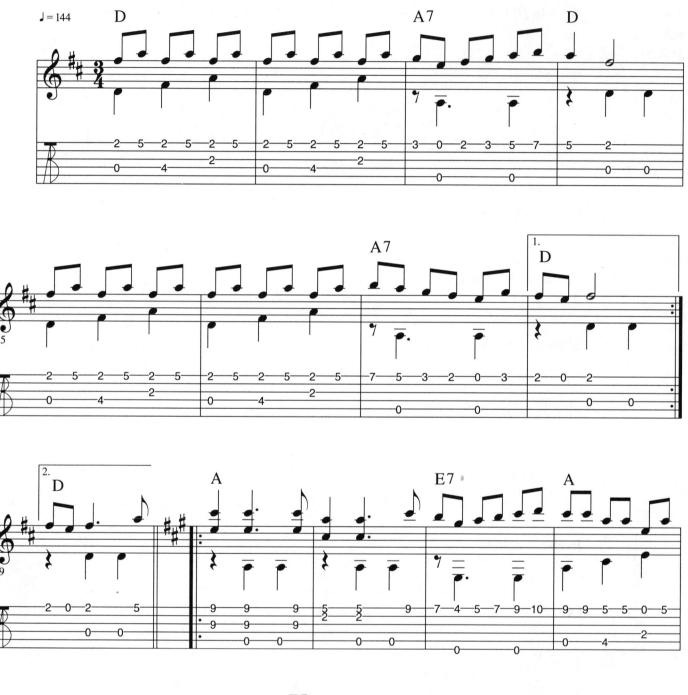

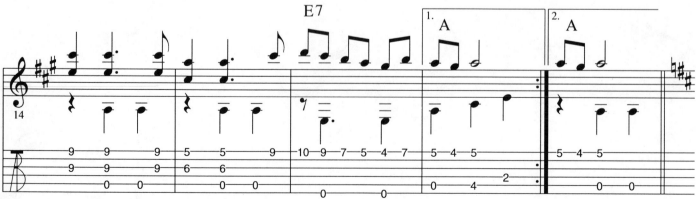

4

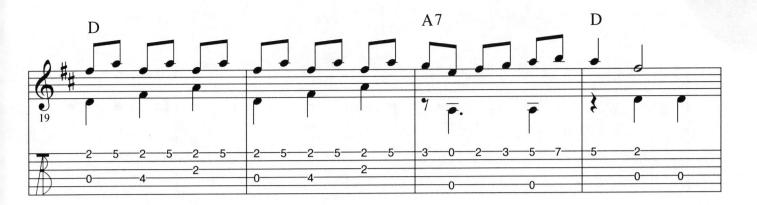

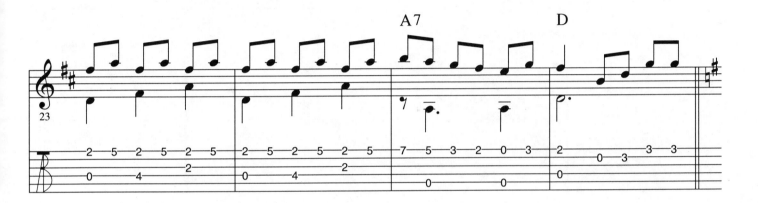

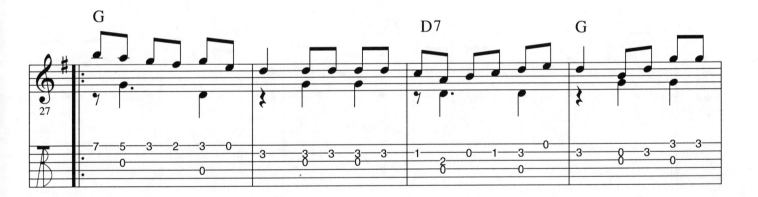

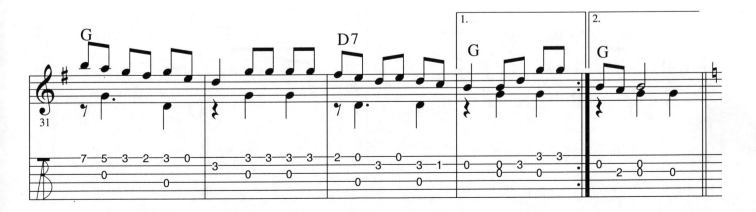

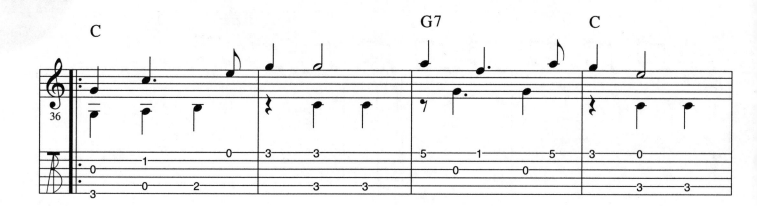

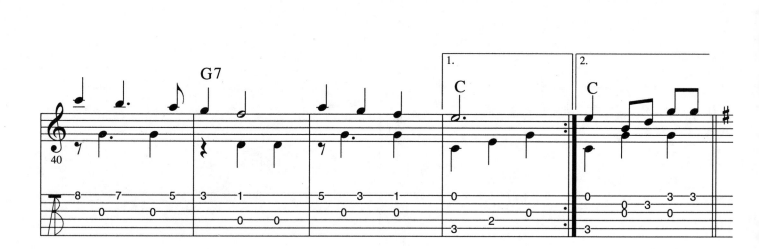

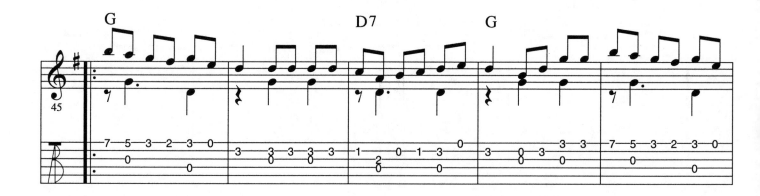

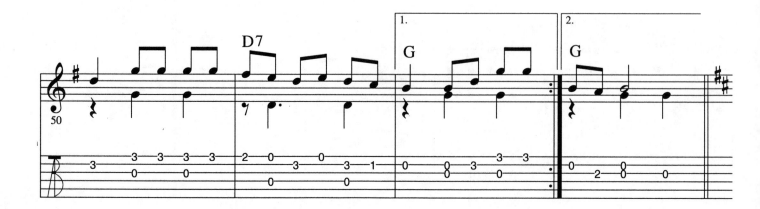

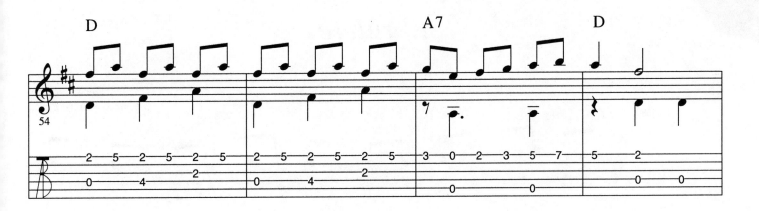

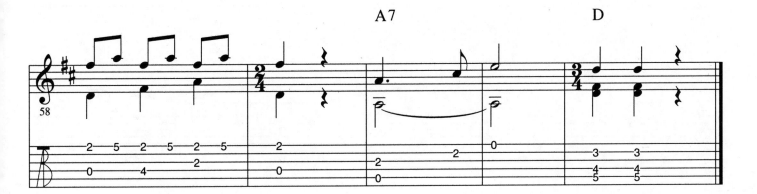

El riflero

Son Jaliscience
adapted by Steve Eckels

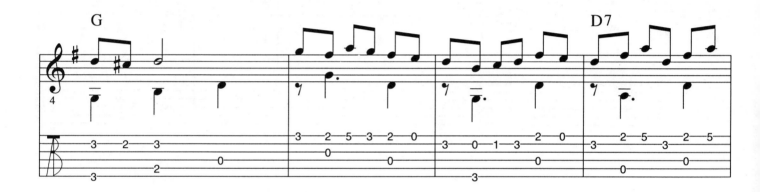

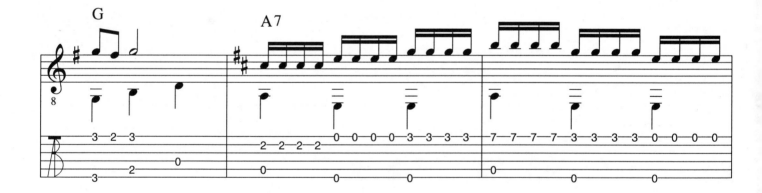

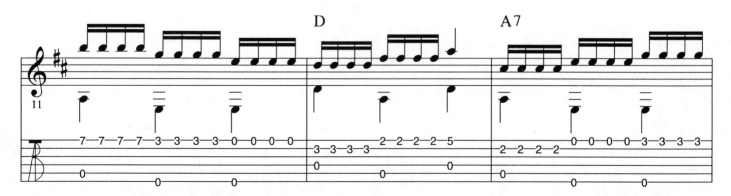

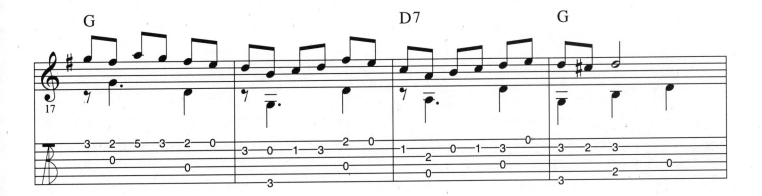

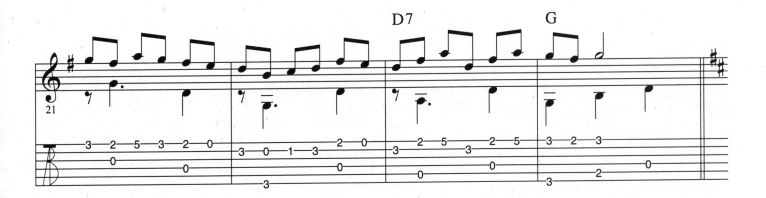

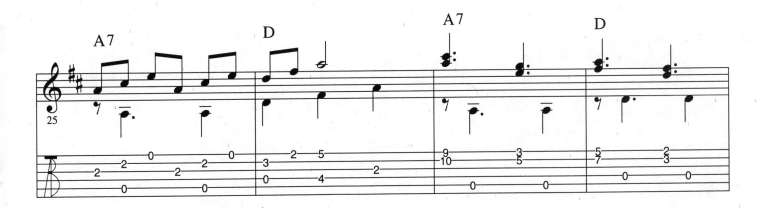

9

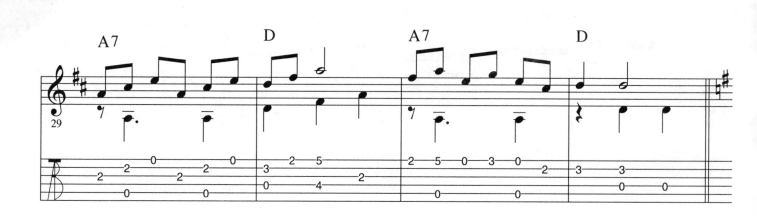

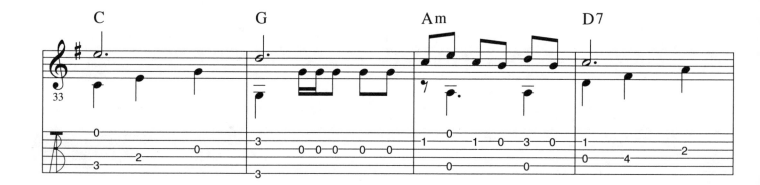

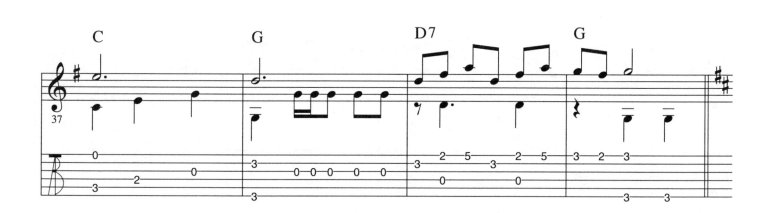

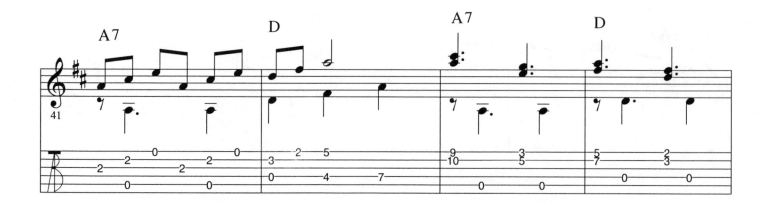

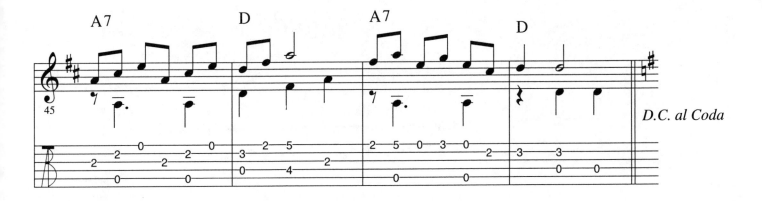

D.C. al Coda

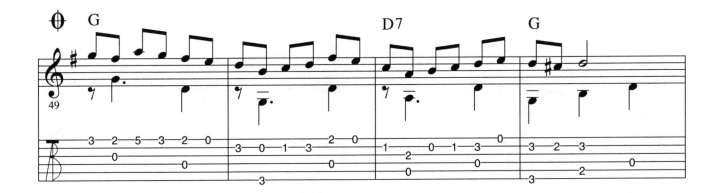

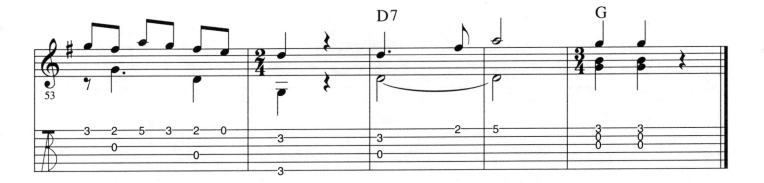

El zopilote mojado

Z. Flores
adapted by Steve Eckels

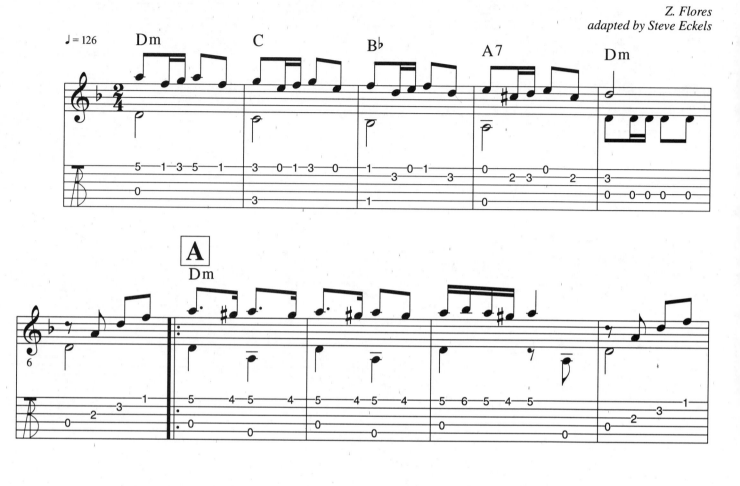

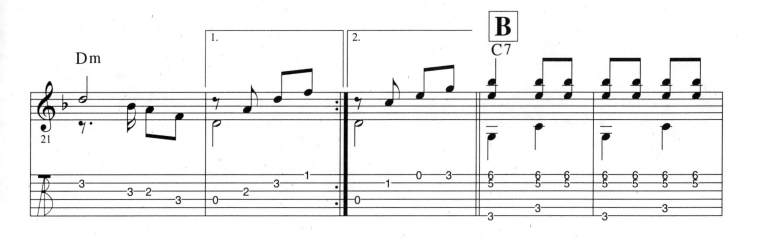

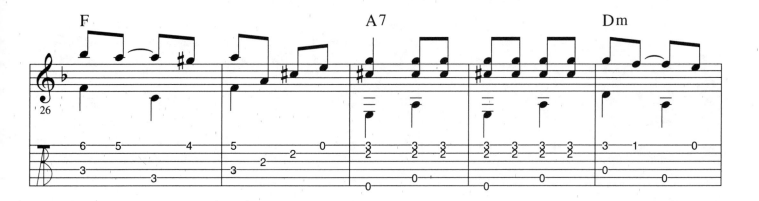

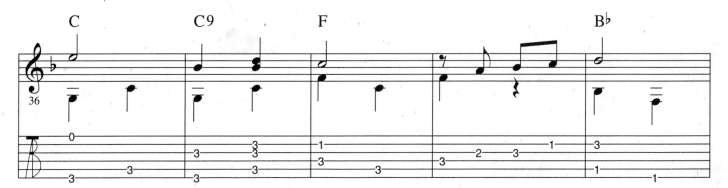

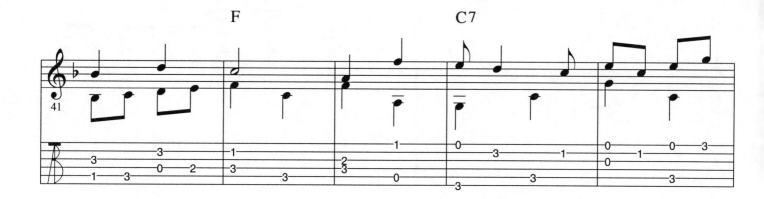

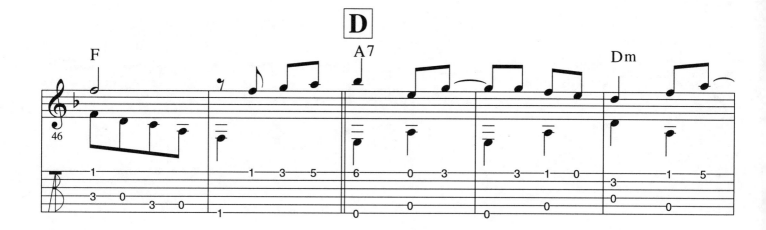

D

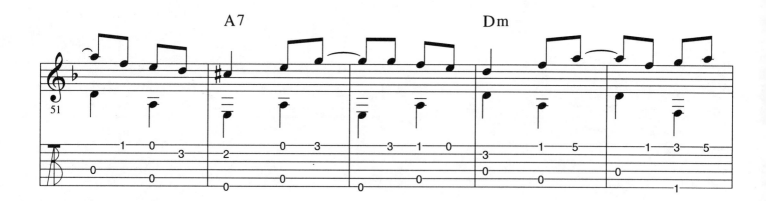

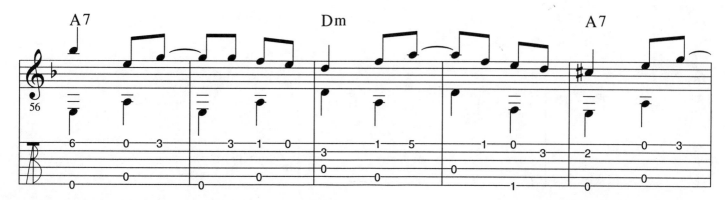

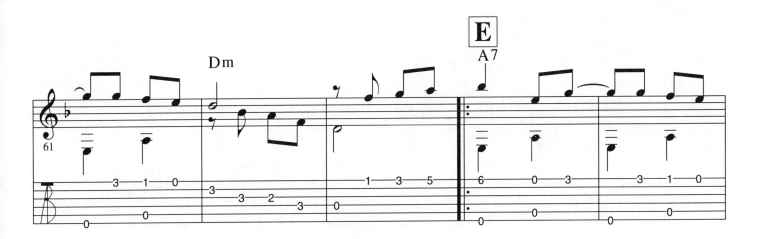

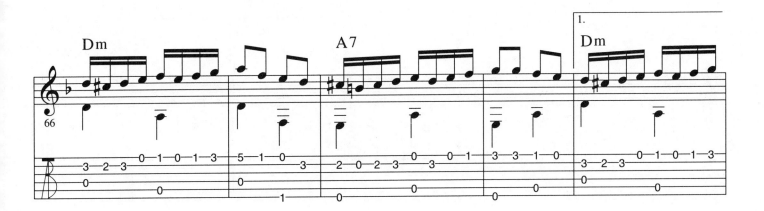

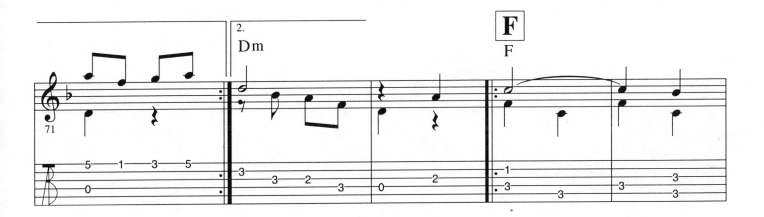

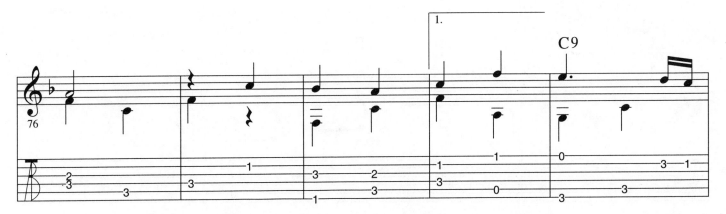

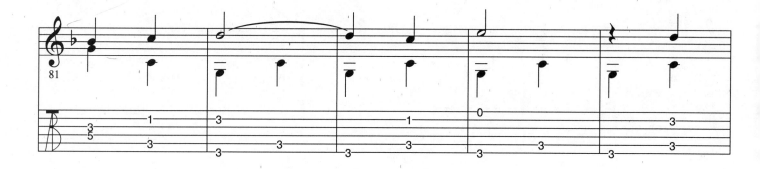

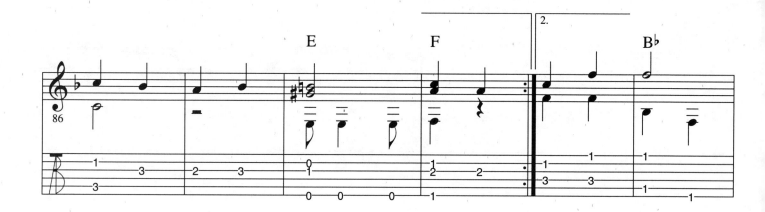

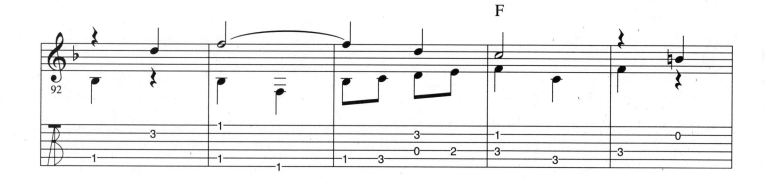

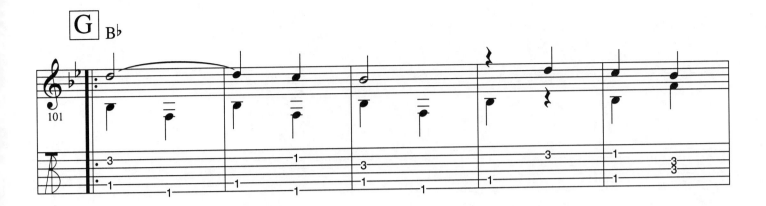

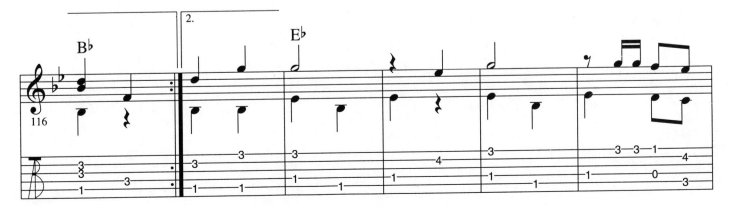

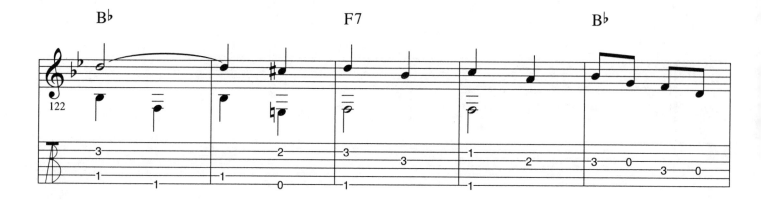

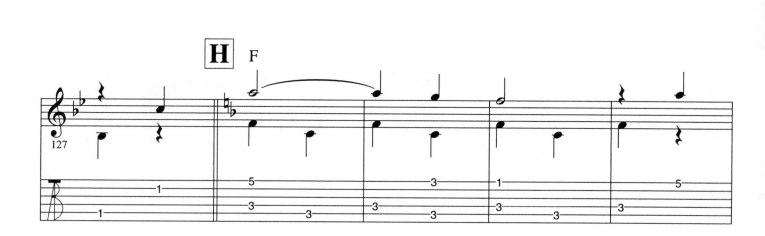

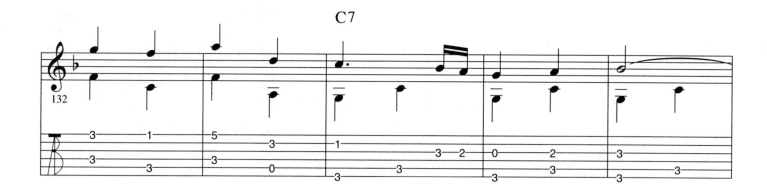

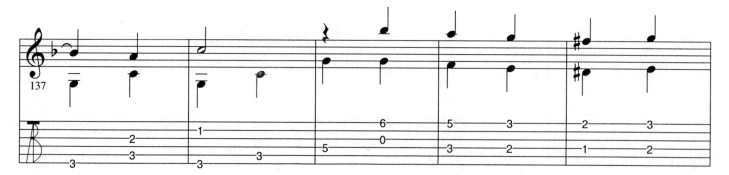

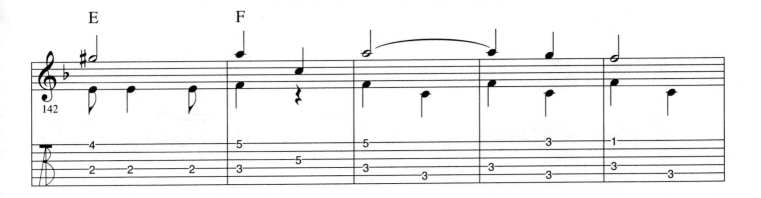

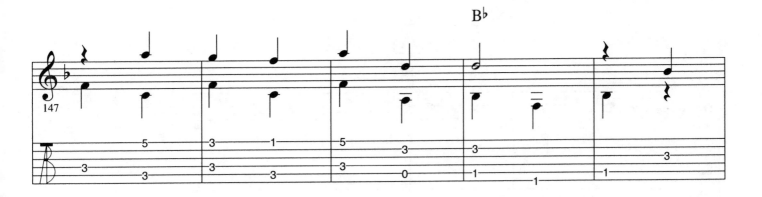

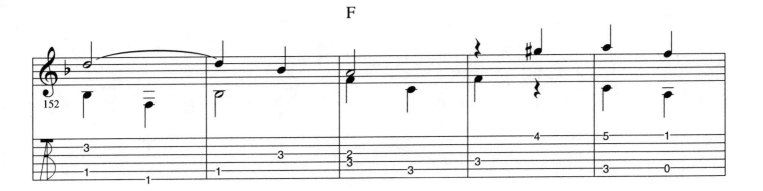

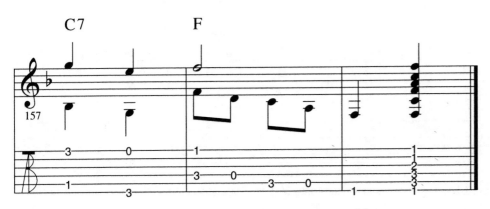

La marcha Zacatecas

G. Godina
adapted by Steve Eckels

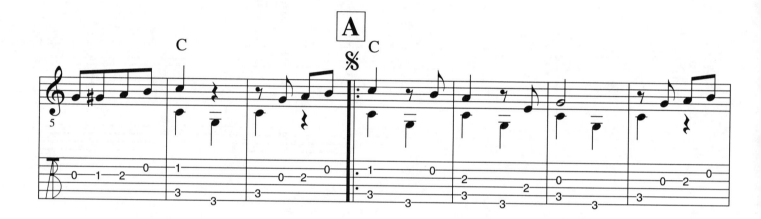

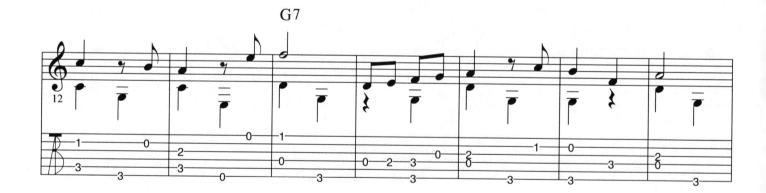

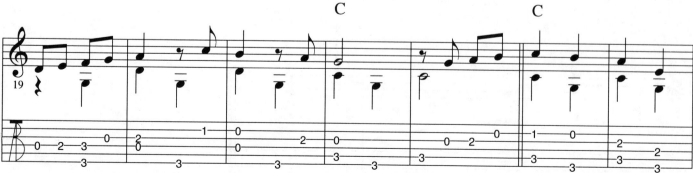

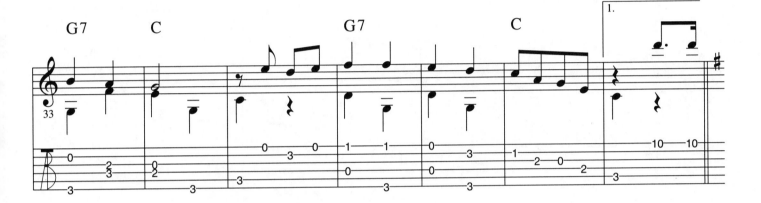

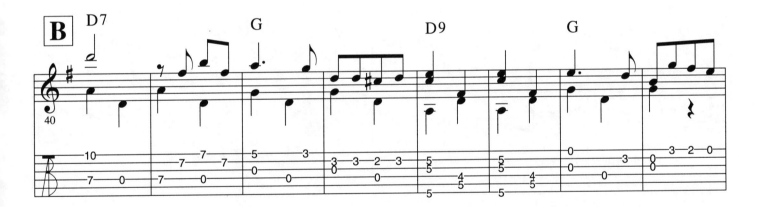

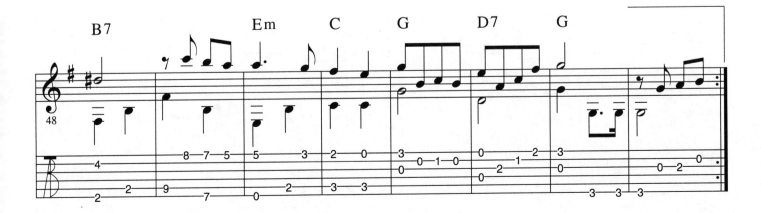

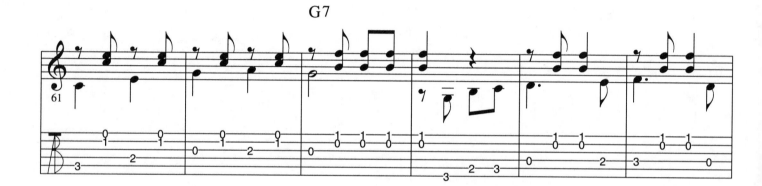

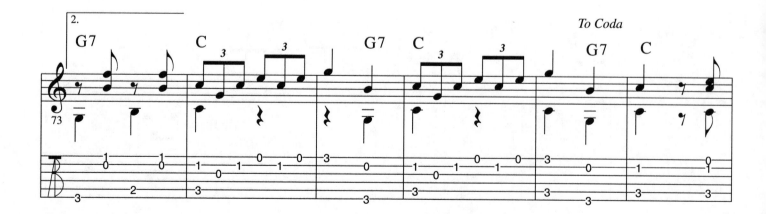

D.S. al Coda

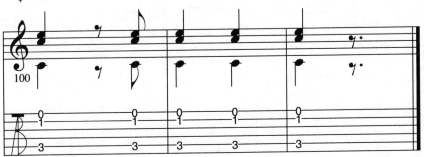

Lindas pachuqueñas

P.D./adapted by Steve Eckels

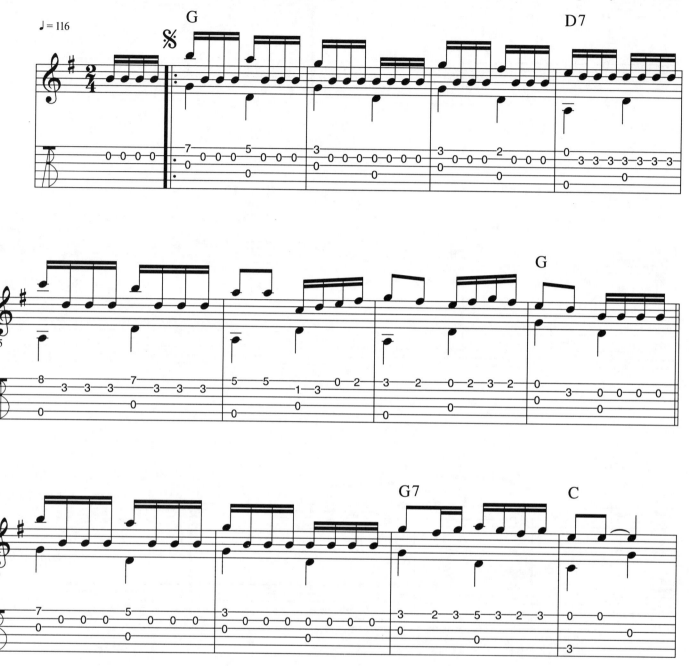

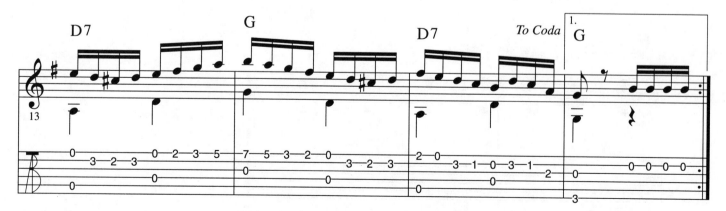

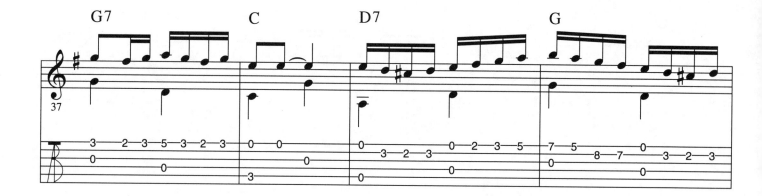

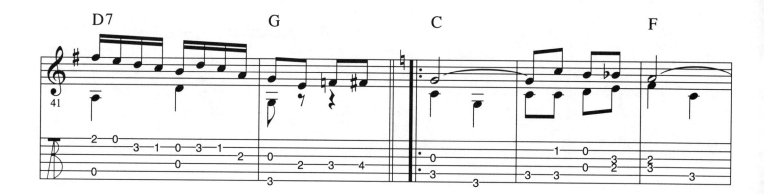

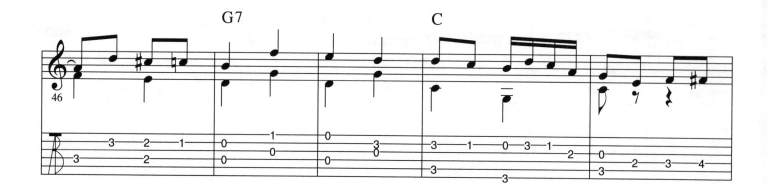

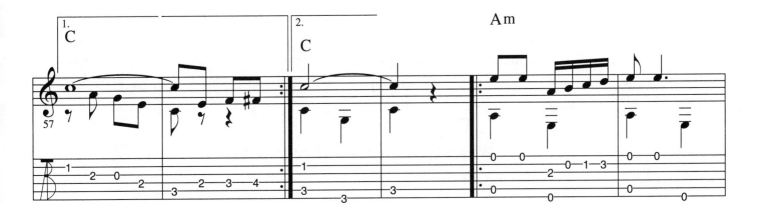

El jarabe Tapatìo

P.D./adapted by Steve Eckels

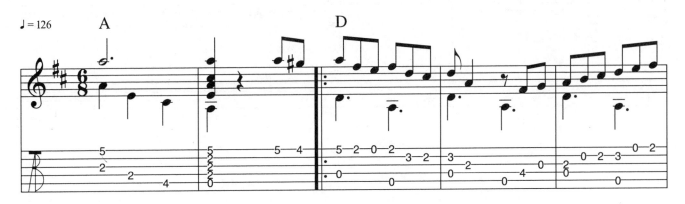

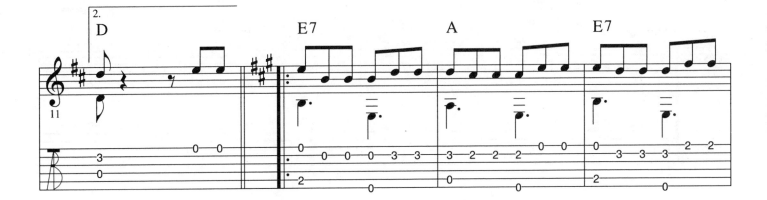

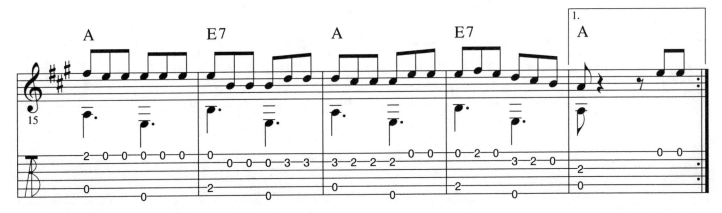

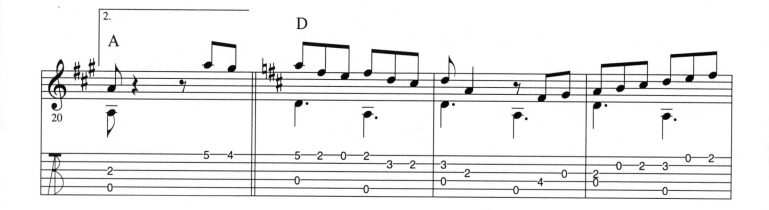

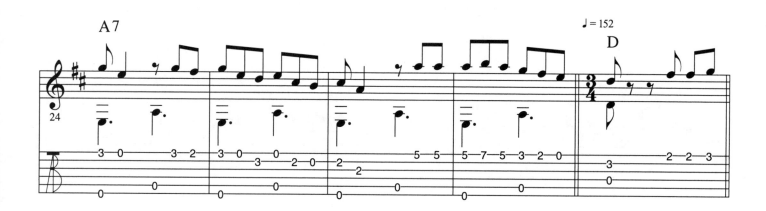

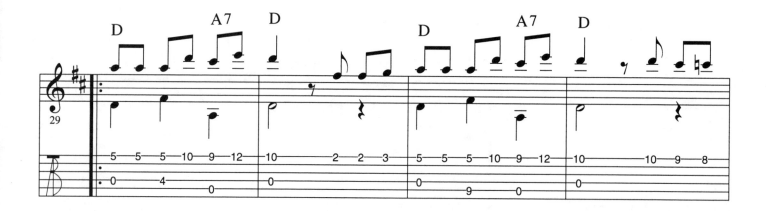

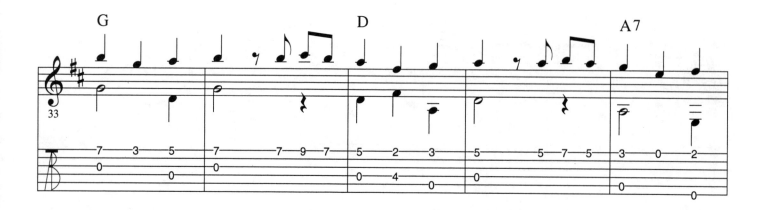

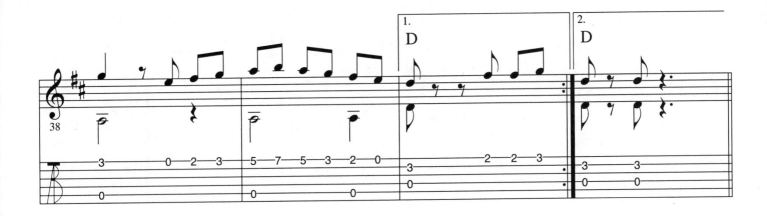

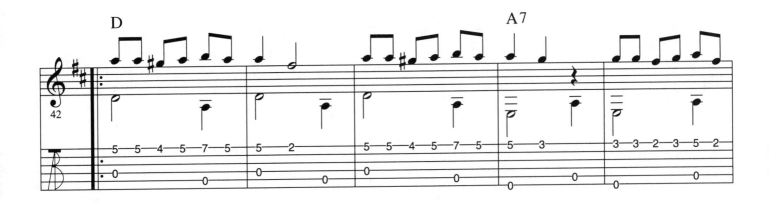

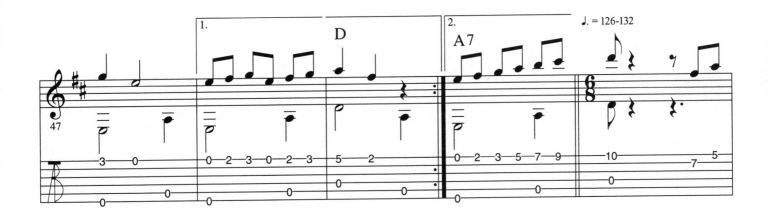

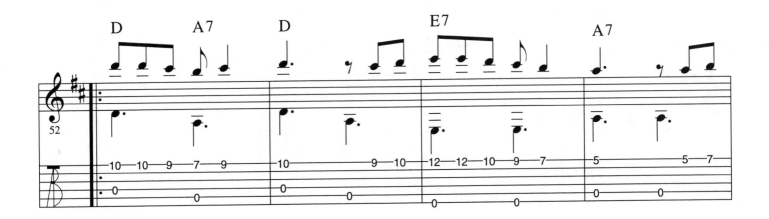

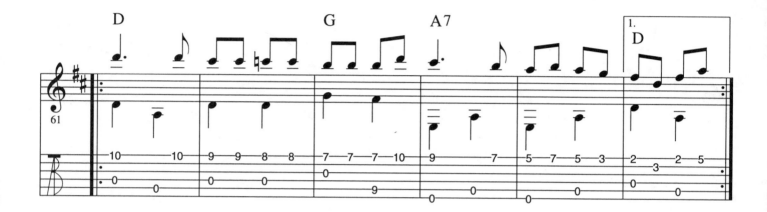

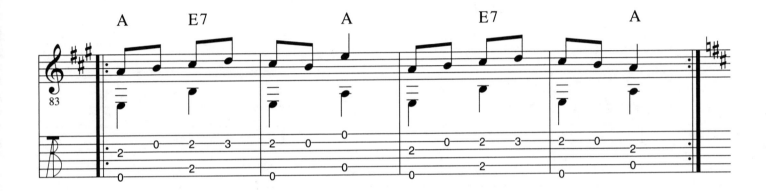

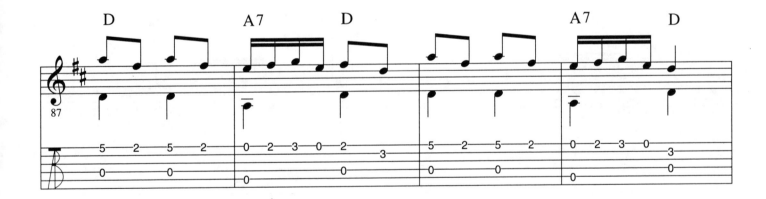

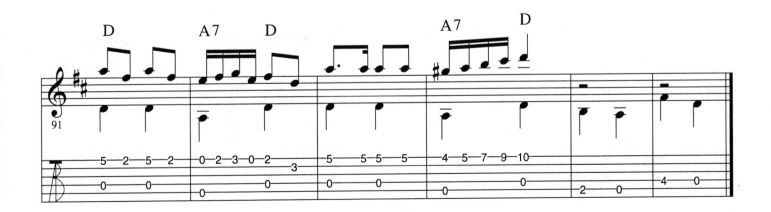

Flor de México

E. Gutiérrez
adapted by Steve Eckels

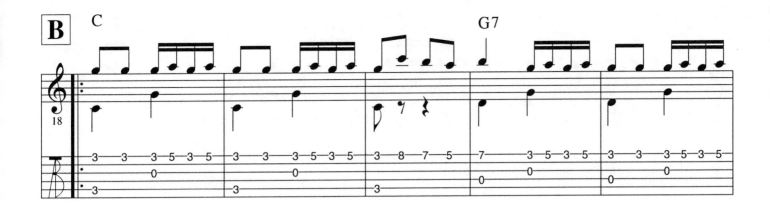

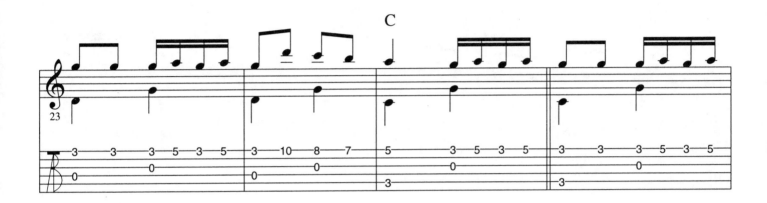

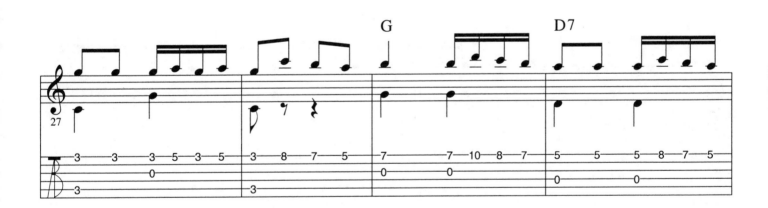

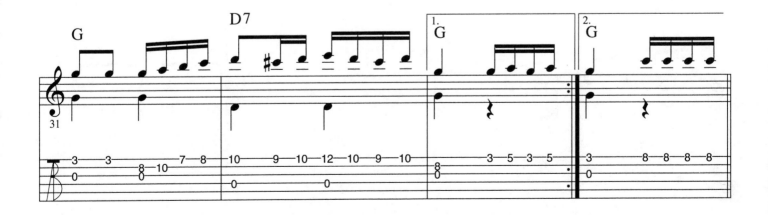

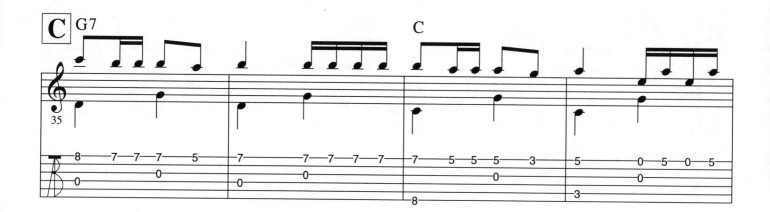

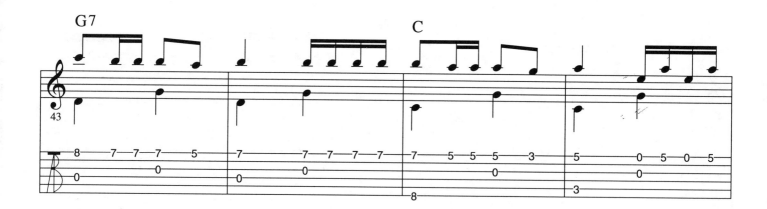

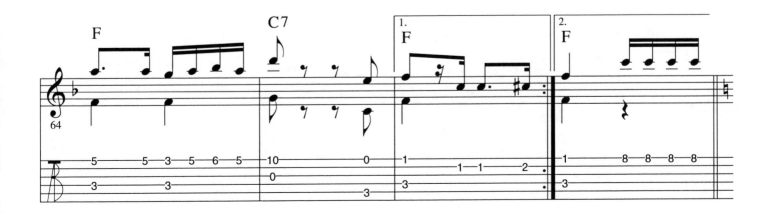

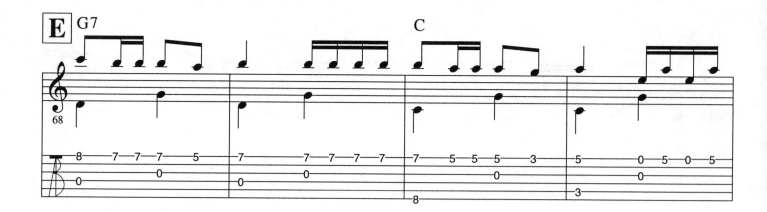

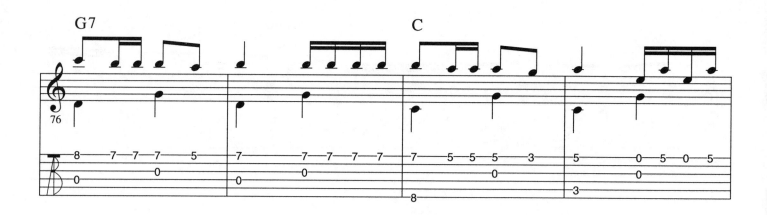

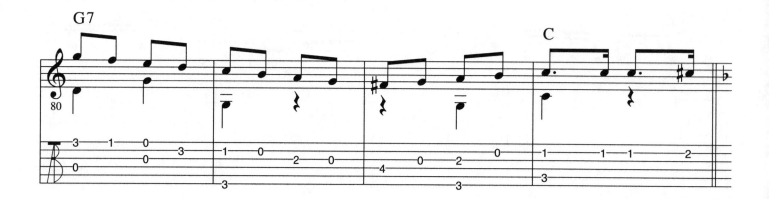

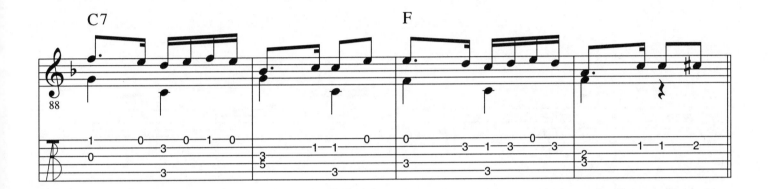

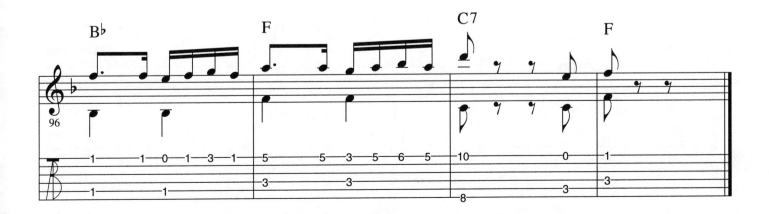

Florecitas Mexicanas

M. Martínez
adapted by Steve Eckels

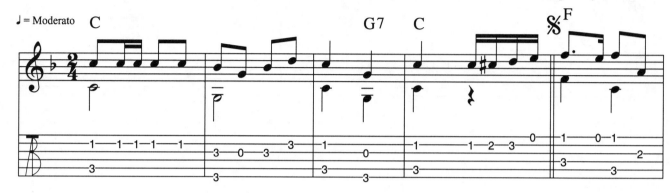

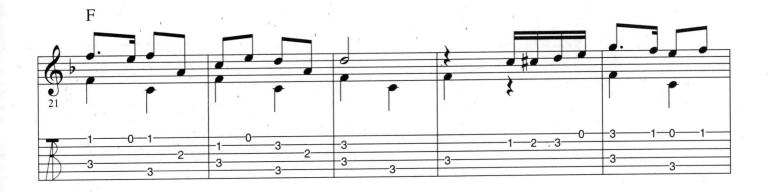

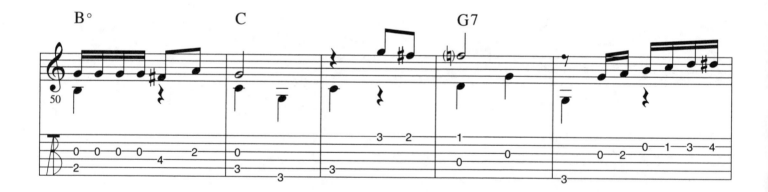

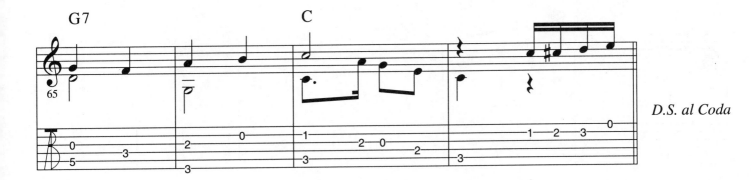

D.S. al Coda

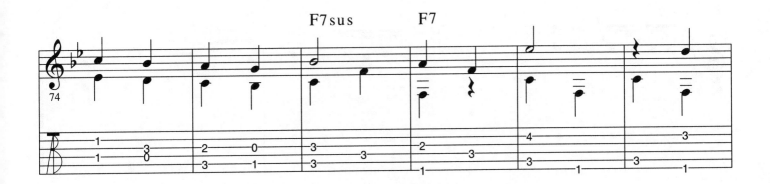

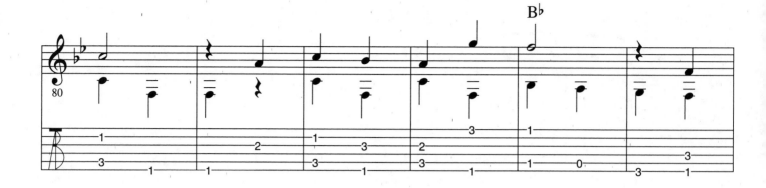

This page has been left blank
to avoid awkward page turns.

Jarabe la botella

P.D./adapted by Steve Eckels

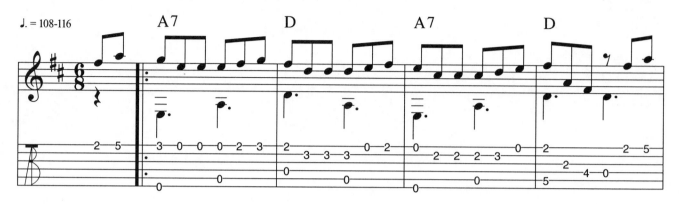

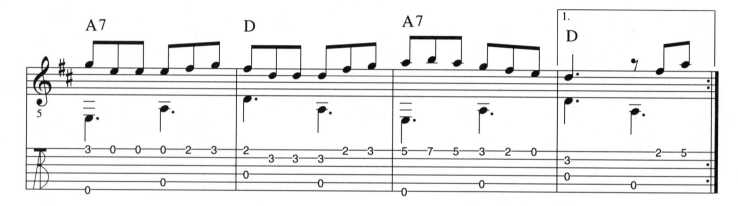

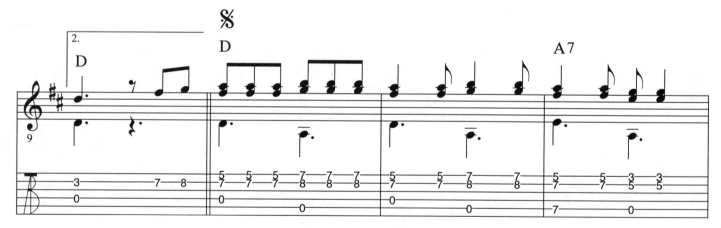

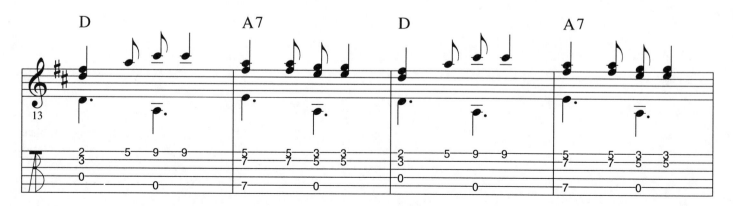

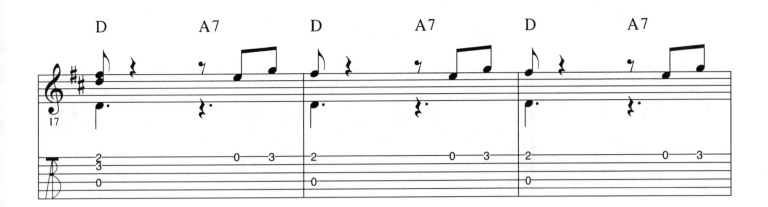

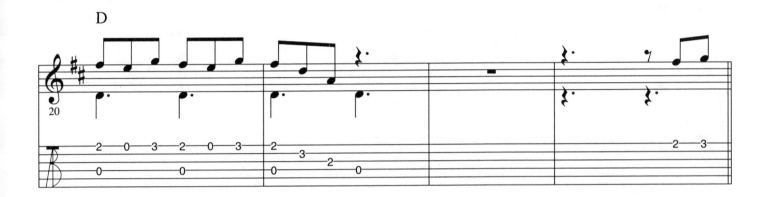

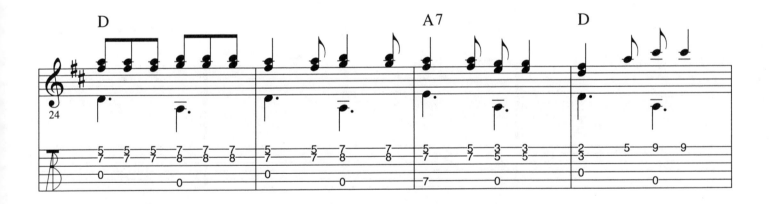

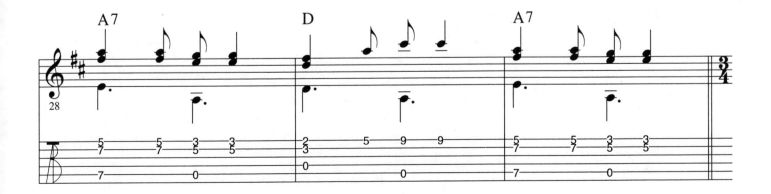

47

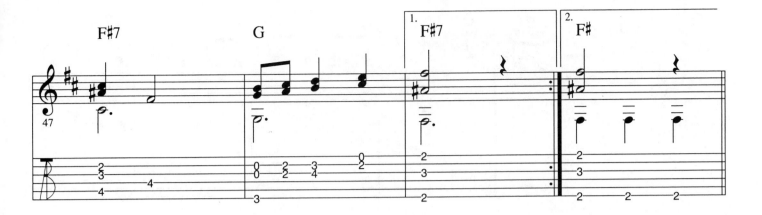

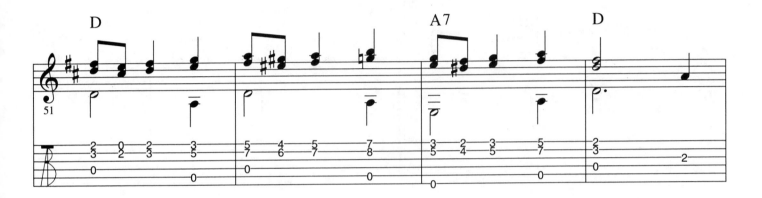

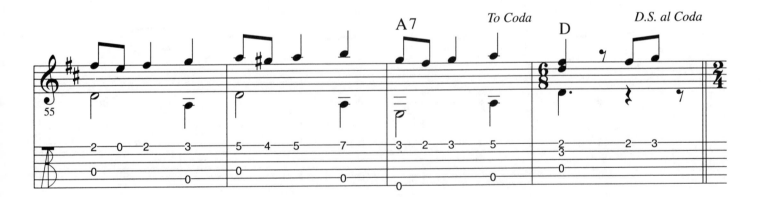

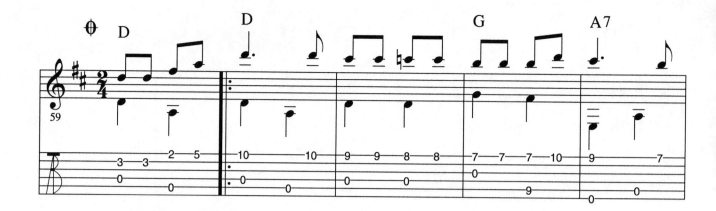

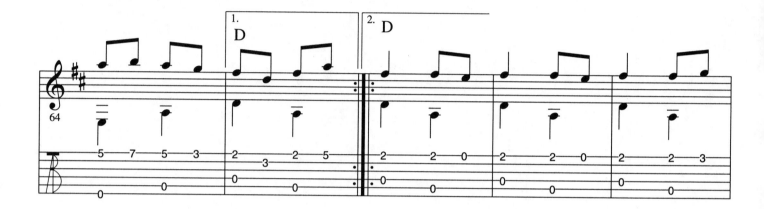

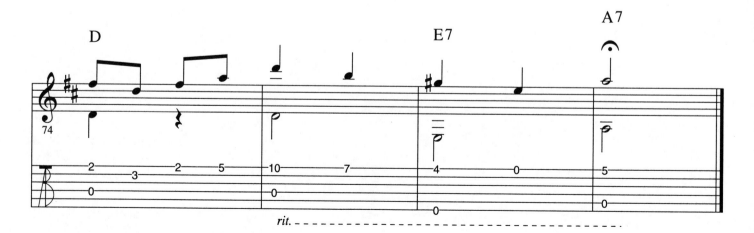

This page has been left blank
to avoid awkward page turns.

La culebra

Fuentes-Vargas
adapted by Steve Eckels

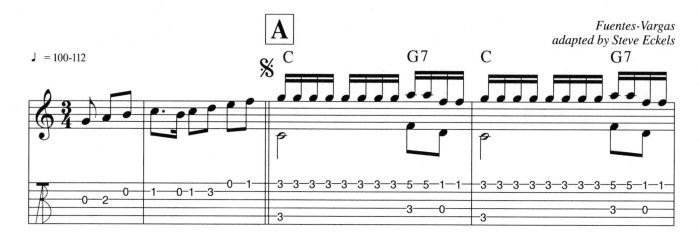

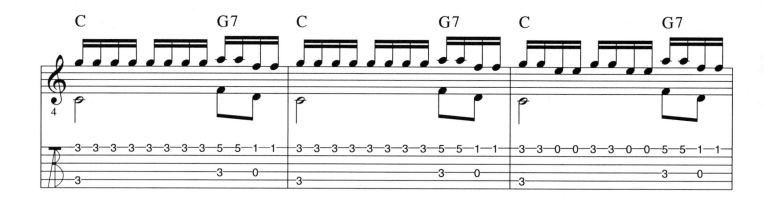

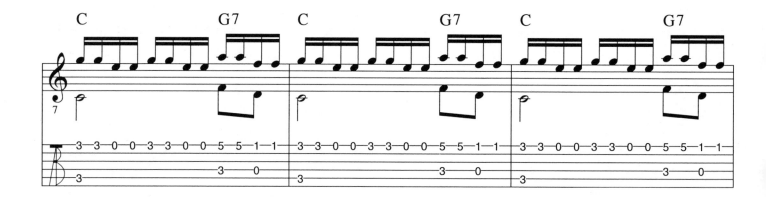

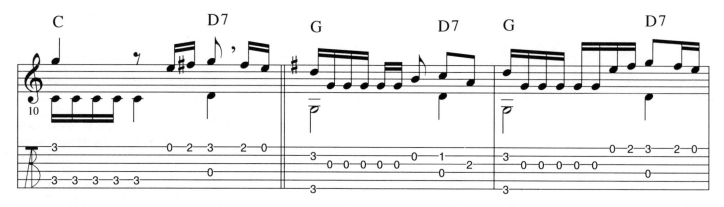

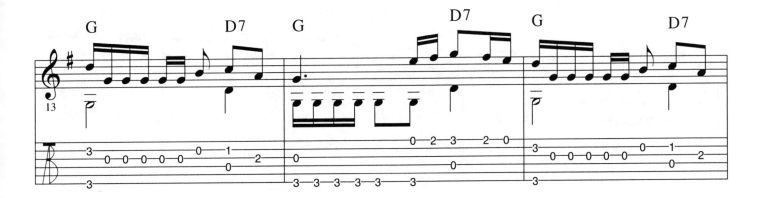

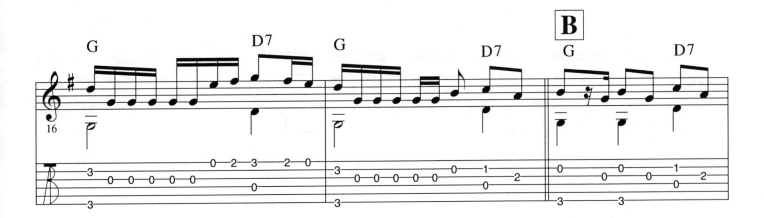

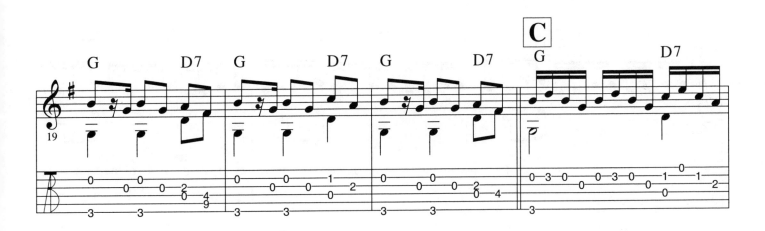

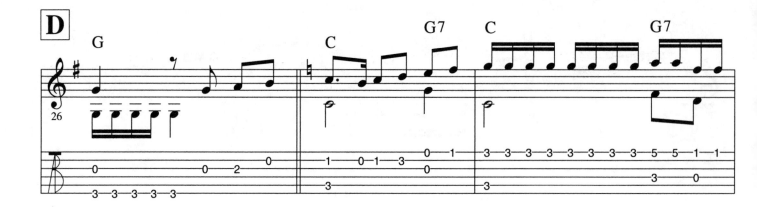

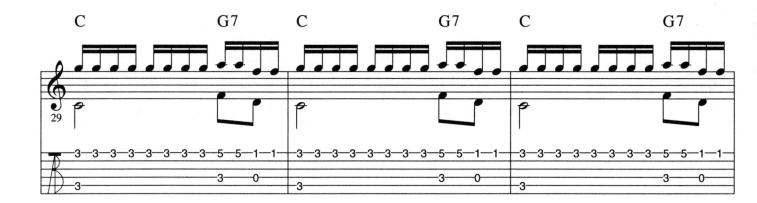

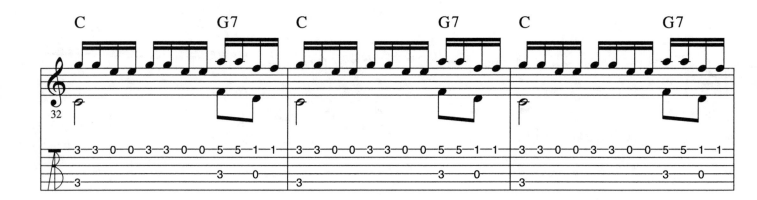

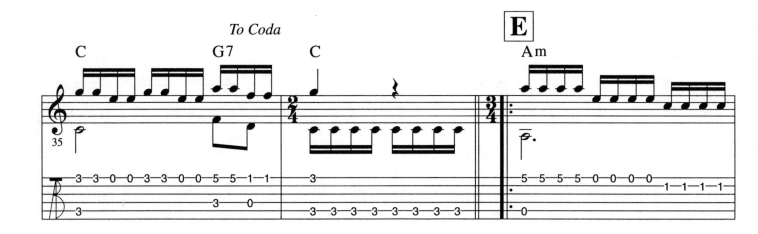

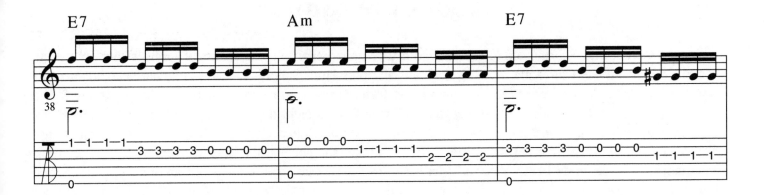

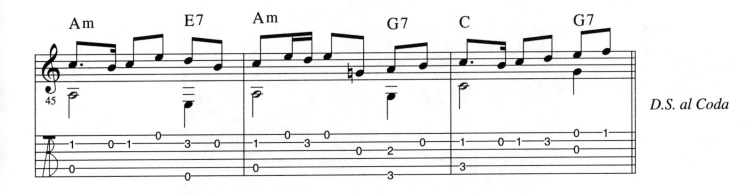

D.S. al Coda

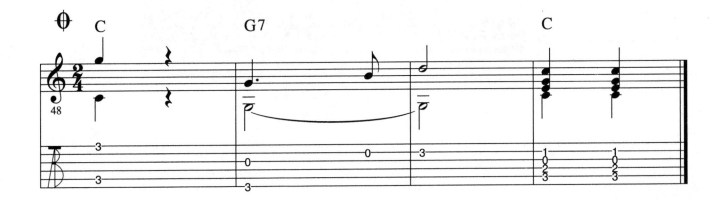

About the Author

Laura Garciacano Sobrino was eight years old when she began playing classical violin at her elementary school in Watsonville, California. A 1972 graduate of Aptos High School, Laura was a charter member of the Santa Cruz County Youth Symphony and enjoyed performing in string quartets. In 1975, while studying for her B.A. at the University of California, she began exploring the mariachi music world as a semi-professional performer, making her one of the first women to enter this predominately male genre. Upon completing her studies, she moved to Los Angeles to perform professionally. There, she became the first woman to play in the groups Mariachi Los Galleros de Pedro Rey and Mariachi Sol de Mexico, both considered among the nation's best. Laura Sobrino was the founding musical director and lead violinist for Mariachi Reyna de Los Angeles, and is currently the Musical Director and violinist for the innovative all-female mariachi show group Mariachi Mujer 2000 (www.mariachimujer2000.com).

Among Mrs. Sobrino's greatest contributions to the mariachi world are her twenty-five plus years of instruction provided to aspiring mariachi musicians, music educators, and other professionals, both young and old; she has offered classes in her home and at colleges, music conferences and other instructional venues. Her experiences as a mariachi instructor inspired the birth of her publishing company, Mariachi Publishing (www.mariachipublishing.com). Her transcriptions have made mariachi music, which for generations was transmitted only by ear, accessible to all. Her transcriptions not only provide a window into the many traditional forms but also capture authentic mariachi style.

Laura Sobrino lives in Whittier, CA with her husband, Dan and their children, Nicte and Nazul. She has her own web site at www.mariachipublishing.com.